Songs of Love & Romance

CONTENTS

ISBN 0-634-00055-1

HAL•LEONARD® CORPORATION

7777 W. BLUEMOUND RD. P.O. BOX 13819 MILWAUKEE, WI 53213

Visit Hal Leonard Online at
www.halleonard.com

(They Long to Be)
CLOSE TO YOU

Lyric by HAL DAVID
Music by BURT BACHARACH

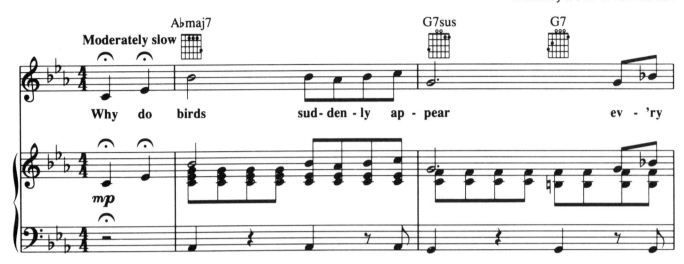

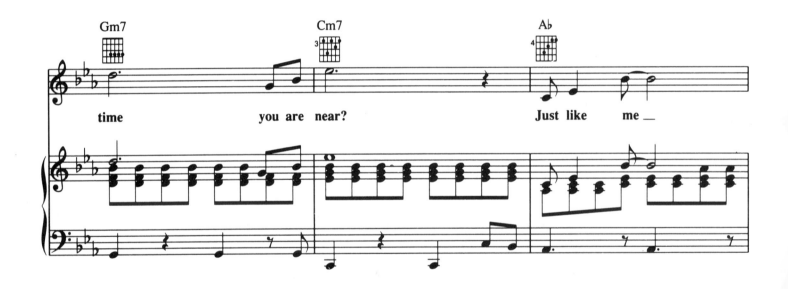

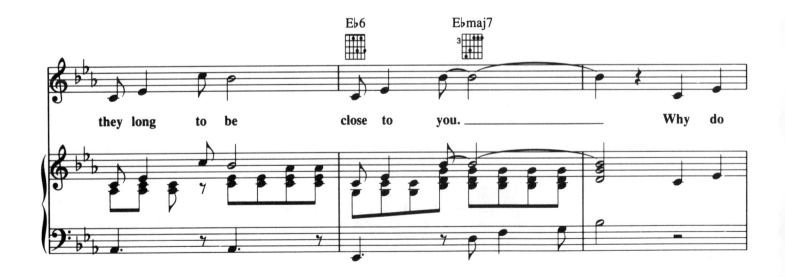

FEELINGS
(¿Dime?)

English Words and Music by MORRIS ALBERT and LOUIS GASTE
Spanish Words by THOMAS FUNDORA

I DREAMED A DREAM
from LES MISÉRABLES

Music by CLAUDE-MICHEL SCHÖNBERG
Lyrics by HERBERT KRETZMER
Original Text by ALAIN BOUBLIL and JEAN-MARC NATEL

IF I FELL

Words and Music by JOHN LENNON
and PAUL McCARTNEY

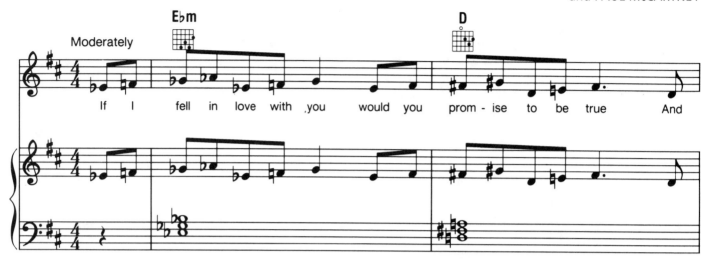

If I fell in love with you would you prom-ise to be true And

help me un-der-stand__ 'Cause I've been in love be-fore And I

found that love was more than just hold-ing hands.__ If I

ISN'T IT ROMANTIC?
from the Paramount Picture LOVE ME TONIGHT

Words by LORENZ HART
Music by RICHARD RODGERS

LET IT BE ME
(Je T'appartiens)

English Words by MANN CURTIS
French Words by PIERRE DeLANOE
Music by GILBERT BECAUD

MCA Music Publishing

THE LOOK OF LOVE

from CASINO ROYALE

Words by HAL DAVID
Music by BURT BACHARACH

25

A MAN AND A WOMAN

(Un Homme et Une Femme)

from A MAN AND A WOMAN

Original Words by PIERRE BAROUH
English Words by JERRY KELLER
Music by FRANCIS LAI

MCA Music Publishing

LOVIN' YOU

Words and Music by RICHARD RUDOLPH
and MINNIE RIPERTON

Lov - - in' you ___ is ea - sy 'cause you're beau - ti - ful,

To Coda

doo doo din doo doo,___ ah.___

CHORUS

No one else___ can make___ me feel___ the co-lours that___ you bring,___

stay with me___ while we___ grow old___ and we___ will live each day in spring-time;

{ 'cause lov - in' you___ has made my life___ so beau-ti-ful, }
{ 'cause lov - in' you___ is ea-sy 'cause___ you're beau-ti-ful, }

MOONLIGHT BECOMES YOU
from the Paramount Picture ROAD TO MOROCCO

Words by JOHNNY BURKE
Music by JAMES VAN HEUSEN

THE NEARNESS OF YOU
from the Paramount Picture ROMANCE IN THE DARK

Words by NED WASHINGTON
Music by HOAGY CARMICHAEL

PEOPLE WILL SAY WE'RE IN LOVE
from OKLAHOMA!

Lyrics by OSCAR HAMMERSTEIN II
Music by RICHARD RODGERS

45

SAVING ALL MY LOVE FOR YOU

Words by GERRY GOFFIN
Music by MICHAEL MASSER

50

SMALL WORLD

from GYPSY

Words by STEPHEN SONDHEIM
Music by JULE STYNE

SOMETIMES WHEN WE TOUCH

Words by DAN HILL
Music by BARRY MANN

SPEAK SOFTLY, LOVE
(Love Theme)
from the Paramount Picture THE GODFATHER

Words by LARRY KUSIK
Music by NINO ROTA

61

STRANGERS IN THE NIGHT
adapted from A MAN COULD GET KILLED

Words by CHARLES SINGLETON and EDDIE SNYDER
Music by BERT KAEMPFERT

Moderately slow

Stran - gers in the night _____ ex - chang-ing glanc - es, won - d'ring in the night _____ what were the chanc - es we'd be shar - ing love _____ be - fore the night was through. _____ Some-thing in your eyes _____ was so in - vit - ing,

MCA Music Publishing

TRUE LOVE WAYS

Words and Music by NORMAN PETTY
and BUDDY HOLLY

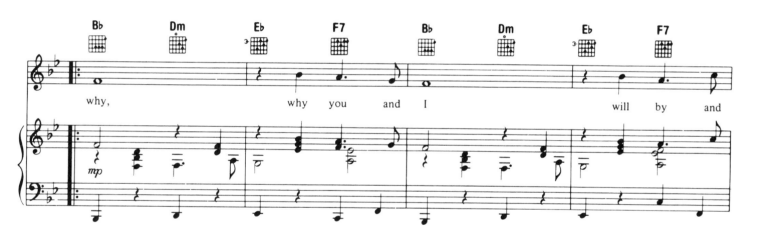

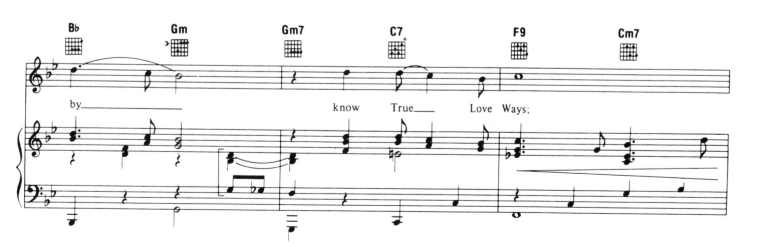

THIS GUY'S IN LOVE WITH YOU

Lyric by HAL DAVID
Music by BURT BACHARACH

TIME AFTER TIME

Words and Music by CYNDI LAUPER
and ROB HYMAN

UNTIL IT'S TIME FOR YOU TO GO

Words and Music by
BUFFY SAINTE-MARIE